020.23   Greene, Carol
GRE   I can be a librarian

13⁶⁰

DATE DUE	BORROWER'S NAME	

01913-9

020.23   Greene, Carol
GRE   I can be a librarian

I CAN BE A
LIBRARIAN

By Carol Greene

Prepared under the direction of Robert Hillerich, Ph.D.

CHILDRENS PRESS ®

CHICAGO

Library of Congress Cataloging in Publication Data

Greene, Carol.
  I can be a librarian.

  Includes index.
  Summary: Describes the work of librarians, the many
different kinds of libraries they work in, and how to
become a librarian.
  1. librarians—Juvenile literature. 2. Libraries—Juvenile
literature. [1. Librarians. 2. Libraries. 3. Occupations]
I. Title.
Z682.G817 1988   020'.23   87-35537
ISBN 0-516-01913-9

Childrens Press,® Chicago
Copyright ©1988 by Regensteiner Publishing Enterprises, Inc.
All rights reserved. Published simultaneously in Canada.
Printed in the United States of America.
    5 6 7 8 9 10 R 97 96 95 94 93

For the helpful people at the
Webster Groves Public Library

PICTURE DICTIONARY

director

librarian

library

library technical assistant (LTA)

card catalog

scroll

tablet

rebound book

branch library

bookmobile

computer

graduate school

The Greek manuscript (above left) was written more than two thousand years ago. The Code of Hammurabi, a set of laws established by Hammurabi, the king of Babylon, was carved onto this stone (above right) eighteen hundred years before the birth of Christ. This Egyptian manuscript (below) was written on papyrus more than four thousand years ago.

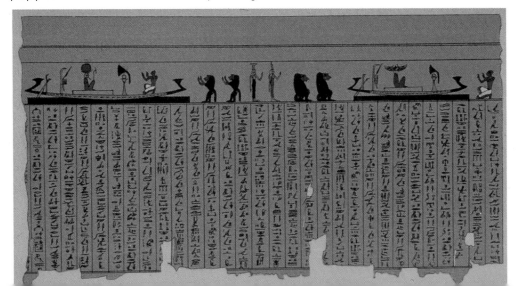

Thousands of years ago, there were no books. But there were librarians!

scroll

These librarians took care of the tablets or scrolls with writing on them. The first books were written out by hand. These books cost a lot of money. Librarians kept them safe.

tablet

library

librarian

Today, librarians work
with books and many
other materials. They
work with different kinds
of people. They must be
able to use many kinds
of machines. That is
because there are many
kinds of libraries.

Some librarians work in
big public libraries. Some

Students may help out in school libraries (left). Bookmobiles (right) bring books to people who do not live close to the library.

drive around in bookmobiles. Some work for schools or universities. Others work for businesses.

A hospital librarian helps sick people find

bookmobile

Doctors and nurses depend on medical libraries for information about the latest research on diseases and medicines.

books to read as they
get well. Sometimes she
or he brings books on
tapes to people.

A medical school
librarian might help a
doctor find information

Computers speed up book checkouts.

about a disease. The
library computer can get
information from other
medical libraries too.
Many librarians work with
computers.

computer

A music librarian can
help people find records
to listen to or musical
scores to play for a
concert.

Children's librarians
often read stories aloud
to groups of children.
Sometimes they show
films.

Some librarians work with maps or art. Others work with facts about law. Still others help people find business information. Even though each librarian may do a different job, in some ways all librarians are the same.

Some librarians order movies (top right) and assist readers with library machines (bottom right). Others work with city records (bottom left) and help find technical information for people (top left).

Librarians help students do research.

All librarians must know
what is in their library.
They must know where
everything is kept. They
must help people find
and use the materials.

Librarians must keep their libraries up-to-date. They must decide what new materials to buy and know where to find them. They must first make sure the library has enough money for the materials. Then they place an order. Sometimes they use a computer to order the books and other materials they need.

After the materials
come in, librarians must
decide where they
belong. Where can
people easily find them?

I can be a librarian

020.23
GRE   Greene, Carol
       I can be a librarian / Childrens Press, © 1988.

       32 p.: col. ill. (I can be books)
       Includes index

       Summary: Describes the work of librarians, the many
       different kinds of libraries they work in, and how to
       become a librarian.

       ISBN 0-516-01913-9
       CP STOCK # 01913-9
       87-35537
       1. Librarians 2. Libraries 3. Occupations I. Title
       II. Title: Librarians

                                                    020.23
                                              Z682.G817 1988
       METRO Catalog Cards   Childrens Press

020.23
GRE   Greene, Carol
       I can be a librarian / Childrens Press, © 1988.

       32 p.: col. ill. (I can be books)
       Includes index

       Summary: Describes the work of librarians, the many
       different kinds of libraries they work in, and how to
       become a librarian.

       ISBN 0-516-01913-9
       CP STOCK # 01913-9
       87-35537
       1. Librarians 2. Libraries 3. Occupations I. Title
       II. Title: Librarians

                                                    020.23
                                              Z682.G817 1988
       METRO Catalog Cards   Childrens Press

Catalog cards (right) are kept in files (left).

The librarian takes care of the card catalog. The cards tell what is in the library. They also tell where in the library those things are kept.

card catalog

17

Librarians also get the materials ready to be used. They may paste on a pocket and put a card in it. They may add a special tape that works with a computer.

When the books and
other materials are ready,
librarians check them out
to people. When people
return the materials,
librarians check them
back into the library.

Librarians must also make sure their materials are in good shape. If a record is scratched, they might order a new one. If a book becomes worn, they might send it out to be rebound.

rebound book

Magazines, newspapers, catalogs, and books are all included in library collections.
Librarians must keep track of the thousands of different items in their libraries.

Librarians often answer questions. Some librarians teach, give speeches, or write for magazines.

Librarians often bring books to people who cannot get to the library. These might include people in nursing homes, prisons, or day care centers.

director

In a small library one person may do many of these jobs. In a large one a staff of librarians work together. Large libraries often have a director. The director may be in charge of several branch libraries too.

branch library

The main reading room of the Library of Congress (left) in Washington, D.C.

graduate school

Most librarians go to
college for four years.
They study a subject
such as literature, music,
or science. Then they go
to graduate school to
study library science.

Some people study for
only one or two years at
a community college.
Then they can become
LTAs, or library technical
assistants.

library technical assistant (LTA)

Librarians enjoy working with people. Every day they answer questions and help people solve their research problems.

Learning foreign languages and computer science can be helpful to a librarian.

People today need a lot of information. But they don't always know where to find it. They need friendly people who can help them.

They need librarians.

WORDS YOU SHOULD KNOW

bookmobile (BOOK•mo•beel)—a small library in a van that moves from place to place

branch library (BRANCH LY • brair•ee)—a smaller library in a different place from the main library

catalog (KAT • ah•lawg)—a collection of cards or computer entries that lists information about library materials, such as title, author, and subject

college (KAH • lij)—a school where people can study after they finish high school

community college (kuh•MYOON•ih•tee KAH•lij)—a college for students who live in the community

computer (kum • PYOO • ter)—an electronic machine that stores and gives back information

director (dih • REK•ter)—the person in charge

graduate school (GRAD • ju•it•SKOOL)—part of a university where people can study after they finish college

information (in • for • MAY•shun)—things to know

librarian (lye • BRAIR • eeyan)—someone who takes care of library materials and helps people use them

library (LYE • brair • ee)—a place where different kinds of information are kept for people to use

library science (LYE • brair • ee SYE • ence)—the study of libraries and how they work

library technical assistant (LYE • brair • ee TEK • nih • kul ah • SISS • tent)— a person who does simple jobs in a library

public (PUHB • lik)—open for use by anyone

rebound (ree • BOWND)—had a new cover put on

scroll (SKROHL)—a roll of paper or animal skin on which people wrote

staff (STAFF)—a group of people who work together

tablet (TAB • lit)—a block of stone on which words or pictures were carved

university (yoo • nih • VER • sih • tee)—an advanced school where people can study after they finish high school or college

INDEX

PHOTO CREDITS

© Cameramann International, Ltd.—9, 10, 13 (top right & left), 17 (right & left), 18, 20, 22 (left), 24, 27

Historical Pictures Service, Chicago—4, (3 photos)

Image Finders: © R. Flanagan—cover, 11, 28 (top)

Journalism Services:
   © Scott Kilbourne—8 (left)
   © Scott Wanner—8 (right)
   © Oscar Williams—13 (bottom left)
   © John Patsch—14 (left), 28 (2 photos)
   © Harvey Moshman—19

© Norma Morrison—7 (2 photos), 13 (bottom right), 14 (right), 16, 22 (bottom & top right), 26

Tom Dunnington—artwork, 2, 3

ABOUT THE AUTHOR

Carol Greene has a B.A. in English Literature from Park College, Parkville, Missouri, and an M.A. in Musicology from Indiana University, Bloomington. She has worked with international exchange programs, taught music and writing, and edited children's books. Ms. Greene now works as a freelance writer in St. Louis, Missouri and has published over sixty books. Some of her other books for Childrens Press include *The Thirteen Days of Halloween, A Computer Went A-Courting,* and *The World's Biggest Birthday Cake* in the Sing-Along Holiday Stories series and *I Can Be a Football Player, I Can Be a Baseball Player,* and *I Can Be a Model* in this series.